Alma Flor Ada • F. Isabel Campoy

Paths

José Martí

Frida Kahlo

César Chávez

Illustrated by Waldo Saavedra and César de la Mora

ALFAGUARA

YOUNG READERS

S A N T I L L A N A

Originally published in Spanish as *Caminos*

Art Director: Felipe Dávalos
Design: Petra Ediciones
Editor: Norman Duarte

Cover: Felipe Dávalos

Santillana USA Publishing Company, Inc.
2105 NW 86th Avenue
Miami, FL 33122

Biography D: *Paths*

ISBN: 1-58105-573-0

The authors gratefully aknowledge
the editorial assistance of Rosa Zubizarreta.

ILLUSTRATORS
FELIPE DÁVALOS: pp. 33
CÉSAR DE LA MORA: pp. 34-46
WALDO SAAVEDRA: pp. 6-27

Printed in Colombia
Panamericana Formas e Impresos S.A.

Contents

To Lourdes Rovira, who inspires creativity and peace. And to all of the teachers who have embraced our invitation to find their own voice.

To Elisa Sanchis, wordsmith and bridge builder.

José Martí

Martí in his study
at 120 Front Street in New York City

Oil portrait by the Swedish painter
Herman Norrman, 1891

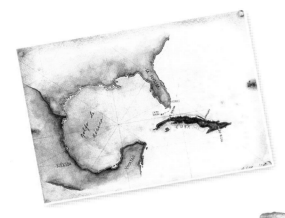

What a joy it is when a newborn child comes into the world. Parents dream that their child be good and strong, brave and noble, intelligent and generous.

On January 28, 1853, in the city of Havana, Cuba, a boy was born who became all of these things and more.

That boy was José Martí Pérez. They called him Pepe. And this is his story.

The island of Cuba is located at the entrance of the Gulf of Mexico. It is very close to Florida and to Mexico. Havana is the capital of Cuba.

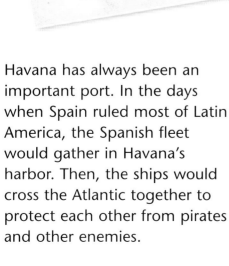

Havana has always been an important port. In the days when Spain ruled most of Latin America, the Spanish fleet would gather in Havana's harbor. Then, the ships would cross the Atlantic together to protect each other from pirates and other enemies.

Jose Martí was born in this humble house at 41 Paula Street.

Pepe's father had to go to work in the countryside for some time. He took Pepe with him. Pepe loved it. He delighted in the green sugarcane fields, the tall royal palms, and the starry nights.

A friend gave Pepe a prize rooster. But his greatest joy was his horse. He took good care of him and taught him how to trot elegantly.

We know about all of this from the letters he wrote home to his mother.

"cada día cría más brío"

7

When Pepe and his father returned to
Havana, Pepe had to get a job in order to
help his family. He was twelve years old.

At first, he worked in a grocery store. Yet,
since he wanted to keep learning, he
looked for work at a school.

Rafael María Mendive
was a true patriot and
a great teacher. He
helped José Martí
continue his studies.

The school principal, Rafael María Mendive,
was a great teacher. He saw that Pepe was very
intelligent and helped him continue his
studies.

At that time, Cuba was a Spanish colony and
the Cuban people were not allowed to govern
themselves. The patriots wanted Cuba to have
its own government and to free the slaves.
Mendive was a patriot, and for that reason he
was put in jail.

One of Mendive's students was not a true patriot.

Pepe and his good friend Fermín Valdez Domínguez wrote this student a letter. They told him that someone who had studied with Mendive ought to love Cuba and love freedom.

José Martí had to cut stone in the lime quarries. It was a terrible punishment.

The letter fell into the authorities' hands. Since the two friends had very similar handwriting, no one knew who had written the letter. To protect Pepe, Fermín said that he had written it. To protect Fermín, Pepe said he was the author of the letter and explained why he believed as he did.

The authorities sent Pepe to prison, sentencing him to hard labor. He was seventeen years old.

9

"Lejanía"

During the trip to Spain, Martí wrote a book about the terrible things that he had seen in jail. Later the book was published in Spain.

After a year in prison, Pepe's father managed to get his sentence changed.

The authorities exiled him from Cuba and sent him to Spain. He would not be allowed to return to Cuba.

The forced labor in the lime quarries, cutting and dragging the stone under the hot sun, was awful. Martí saw young boys and old men suffering terribly.

EN ESTAS CANTERAS SUFRIERON TRABAJOS FORZADOS MUCHOS CUBANOS POR EL HONROSO DELITO DE QUERER LA LIBERTAD DE SU PATRIA. EN ESTAS CANTERAS TRABAJÓ Y SUFRIÓ JOSE MARTÍ.

"Hora de lluvia"

In Spain, José Martí found Fermín Valdez Domínguez. Both friends studied law at the University of Zaragoza. Pepe published a book denouncing the horrible treatment of political prisoners.

Martí discovered that Spain, his parents' and grandparents' country was a beautiful land. He met many good people and came to see that some Spaniards loved freedom as much as he did.

Martí decided to devote his life to the fight for freedom, against tyranny, against injustice, and against those who harmed the poor.

Martí discovered the beauty of Spain. He learned that there are good people everywhere.

Martí lived in Madrid for a few months but most of his time in Spain was spent in Zaragoza, the capital of the Aragón region.

The Spanish authorities would not allow José Martí to return to Cuba. His parents and sisters moved to Mexico. Pepe went to Mexico to be with them.

He lived in Mexico.
He lived in Guatemala.
He lived in Venezuela.

Wherever Martí lived, he read and studied. He also worked a great deal teaching and writing.

Wherever he went, he made good friends. He worked to bring about freedom everywhere. Finally, he came to live in the United States, in New York City.

Martí worked long hours. He taught, he translated, and he wrote.

"El maestro en New York"   N. S. Meredith

With those who live in poverty
I choose to cast my lot.
The humble mountain brook
pleases me more than the mighty sea.

Martí wrote constantly. He wanted people to recognize the beauty of life. He wanted to help others find goodness within themselves. He worked tirelessly to encourage Cubans to join together and help each other.

In New York, Martí started a night school for working people. At that time, there were few schools of this kind.

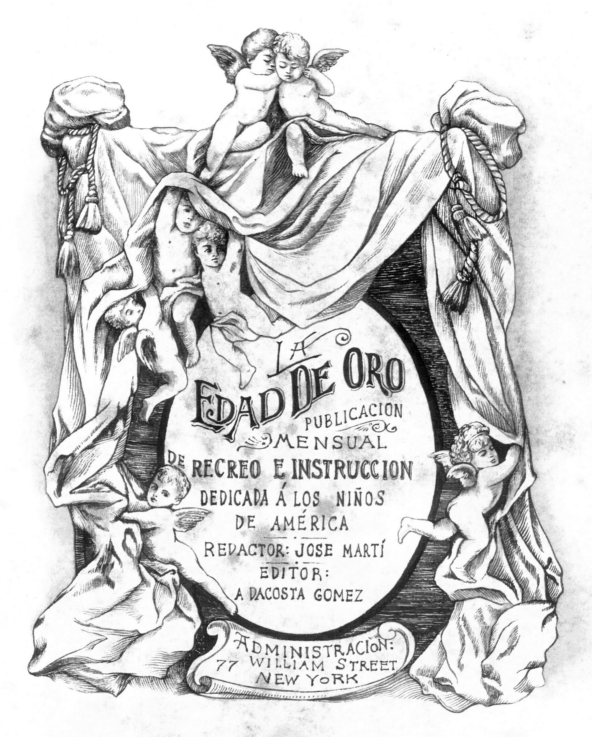

Martí loved children very much. He wrote *La Edad de Oro* (The Golden Times) for all the boys and girls of the Americas. This magazine included stories, poems, and articles. It has been published in book form many times in various countries. In it you will find the beautiful poem "The Rose-colored Shoes."

Martí traveled throughout the United States. He spoke wherever there were groups of Cubans, in Tampa, Key West, Philadelphia, New York.

He spoke of Cuba and of freedom. He spoke about the need to unite in order to achieve Cuban independence.

Martí did not like violence. He did not want war. He loved peace. But he felt that at times it is necessary to fight. Instead of a war between Cubans and Spaniards, he saw the need to fight for freedom for all, for the good of all.

Everyone who heard Martí was moved. They knew they were listening to an extraordinary man.

Martí managed to return to Cuba in 1895. He had succeeded in inspiring the old patriots, who were weary of fighting, to join forces and renew the struggle for Cuba's independence.

In a small Dominican town named Montecristi, lived General Máximo Gómez, who had fought for many years to liberate Cuba. Martí went to see him and together they made plans.

Martí and Máximo Gómez decided to go to Cuba. They hired a ship to take them near the Cuban coastline. The ship lowered a rowboat for Martí and Gómez to go ashore.

It was a stormy night. The small rowboat seemed on the verge of capsizing. The men rowed desperately and finally made it to shore, at a place called Playitas.

Martí landed on the beach at Playitas in Oriente. He had finally returned to the land where he was born.

"No siento como quien va a correr riesgo"...

The renowned Dominican patriot Máximo Gómez fought for Cuban's independence with great dedication.

I wish that after I die
with no country, yet with no master
on my tombstone there lay
a handful of flowers,
    and my homeland banner.

Every day he wrote in his journal. He also wrote beautiful letters to his friends.

The three Greater Antilles, Cuba, Hispaniola, and Puerto Rico, were united in the fight for their freedom.

Martí and the few patriots who accompanied him walked through the mountains. Martí's eyes lit up with joy at each plant he saw and each leaf he recognized. How dearly he loved the Cuban countryside! How well he remembered it! How familiar it was to him!

One afternoon, they were surprised by a column of enemy soldiers. Martí was at the front of the group. His white horse shone brightly in the light of the setting sun. He was shot and fell off his horse mortally wounded and died shortly afterwards. It was May 19, 1895. Martí, who had devoted his life to humanity and to fighting for Cuban independence, died defending his ideals. His death was an inspiration for Cubans to continue to struggle for independence.

José Martí wrote these verses:

Send me not into the dark
to die as traitorous heart;
I am good and, by that right,
I wish to die in sun's bright light.

This poem by Martí is very well known. You may have heard these words sung to the music of "Guantanamera." Martí invites us to love others, be they friends or enemies.

THE WHITE ROSE

I carefully tend a white rose
in both January and July
for the true friend who offers
an honest and loyal hand.

And for the cruel one
who tears from me
my moving and beating heart
I tend neither thistle nor thorn bush
but instead a white, white rose.

The Cuban countryside that Martí loved so much.

This extraordinary man called José Martí is known to Cubans as "The Apostle." His life and his words are an example for all Latinos and Latin Americans, for everyone who speaks Spanish, and for all who love goodness and justice.

Frida Kahlo

Frida Kahlo in 1939
Photograph by Nickolas Muray

Frida was born in Coyoacán on July 6, 1907.

Frida lived in the Blue House with her parents and three sisters.

In the summer months, storms bring heavy rains to the high plateau of Anáhuac, where Mexico City is located.

On July 6, 1907, one of those stormy days, Frida Kahlo was born in the Blue House, in the neighboring city of Coyoacán.

The Blue House had a big central patio, where Frida played with her younger sister Cristina.

Two older sisters, Matilde and Adriana, helped their mother clean and tidy up the house.

In the afternoons, the mother and her four daughters would sit in the patio to do their sewing and embroidery.

At one end of the patio, Frida's father, Guillermo Kahlo, had his photography studio. Those were happy and prosperous days for the Kahlo family.

Frida at age three. This picture was taken by her father, Guillermo Kahlo.

That happiness did not last forever.

Frida's father became sick.
When Frida was six, she became ill too. She had polio. These problems brought Frida and her father closer.

She often went out with him when he went to take photographs of buildings. Sometimes Mr. Kahlo would collapse, and Frida had to ask for help.

Polio affected Frida's right leg. It was thinner than her left leg. But Frida persistently exercised and played sports to strengthen her thin leg.

Frida and her father were always together.

Here are the four Kahlo sisters: Cristina, Adriana, Matilde, and Frida.

Portrait of My Father, Wilhelm Kahlo, 1952
Frida Kahlo

This is Frida's father. She painted him with great affection.

21

Frida went to primary school in Coyoacán.

She had many girl friends with whom she would play after school around town or by the river. She always covered her thin leg with long stockings or pants.

At fifteen, she entered high school.

The school was in Mexico City, one hour away from Coyoacán. Every day she traveled back and forth by bus.

Frida was very intelligent and found friends who could understand her. She became friends with a group of young men who were known as the Cachuchas.

The Cachuchas would meet in the library to study and to do their homework. The leader of the group, Alejandro Gómez Arias, was Frida's best friend.

She continued to hide her leg by wearing long skirts or pants.

This is Alejandro Gómez Arias, a good friend of Frida's.

Frida loved to play.
Frida loved to laugh.
Frida loved to live.
But, most of all, she loved
to dream.

Frida in Coyoacán, 1927
Frida Kahlo

The Bus, 1929
Frida Kahlo

One day, Frida was in the bus on her way to school. As usual she was talking with her friend Alex, when a terrible accident happened.

A trolley crossed in front of the bus, and Frida was badly injured. Alex stayed by her side until the ambulance arrived.

This is a drawing of the accident, done by Frida in 1926.

Frida had several fractured bones, and she had lost a lot of blood. Nobody in the hospital thought that she would survive. She was there for a month, and her friends often visited her.

When she was released from the hospital, her friends continued to travel to Coyoacán to visit her, but eventually they became tired of the hour-long bus ride.

Self-Portrait Wearing a Velvet Dress, 1926
Frida Kahlo

Frida never finished her schooling. This was when she began painting.

Frida's mother, Matilde Calderón, had a small easel built to hang above her daughter's bed. She placed a mirror above Frida's bed. Looking at herself, Frida painted self-portraits again and again. Painting kept her occupied. For two years, she fought for her life.

When she was better, she showed her paintings to a famous muralist, Clemente Orozco. He in turn showed them to Diego Rivera.

Diego Rivera was a famous painter. He painted murals on the walls of public buildings. His drawings were very beautiful. When he saw Frida's drawings he said,

"Your drawings are as beautiful as you."

She continued to show him her drawings, and he began to court her. They were married on August 21, 1929.

Frida and Diego, 1931
Frida Kahlo

Diego Rivera was a famous painter of murals. Diego and Frida loved each other.

Frida Kahlo, c. 1931
Photo by Imogen Cunningham

One year later, Diego and Frida moved from Mexico City to San Francisco, California, where Diego was to paint several murals.

Frida walked the streets of San Francisco dressed in her long Mexican skirts. People stopped to stare at her.

She spent her days visiting museums and riding the streetcars up and down the hills of the city. She often went to stores in Chinatown, where she would find silk cloth to make her long skirts.

In San Francisco she met Dr. Leo Eloesser, a doctor who became her advisor and friend for the rest of her life.

Dr. Eloesser loved to go sailing in San Francisco Bay. Frida had never seen his boat, but she painted him with a model sailboat.

Portrait of Dr. Leo Eloesser, 1931
Frida Kahlo

Diego and Frida, 1929

From San Francisco, Frida and Diego went to Detroit. In Detroit, Diego painted murals depicting the workers in the automobile factories.

Frida's mother died. The death of Matilde Calderón was very sad for everyone, especially for Frida's father, who loved her very much.

Self-Portrait on the Border Between Mexico and the United States, 1932
Frida Kahlo

Frida's parents on their wedding day.

Detroit Industry, 1932-1933
Diego Rivera

Diego and Frida went from Mexico to California and then Detroit. They returned to Mexico when Frida's mother died.

Murals are large paintings done on the walls of buildings.

Diego and Frida went to New York several times.

In New York, they met painters and other artists. Diego was painting a large mural. Frida visited him daily at noontime. She carried a basket with lunch for him.

In the basket, Frida always put flowers and letters reminding him how much she loved him. Frida remembered how the women in the Mexican countryside would bring food to their husbands at work in the fields. She did the same for her husband in New York.

Diego and Frida loved each other very much.

In New York, Frida met Nickolas Muray, a photographer. He took some of the best pictures of her from that time. Frida also had an exhibit of her own work. One of her paintings from that time is entitled *My Dress Hangs Here* (1933).

In New York, Frida would visit Diego every day at his work site. She always took him his lunch in a basket.

From New York, Frida went to Paris. She was very successful there. At that time, many talented poets, painters, and artists lived in Paris. They often met to talk and exchange ideas about their work. Among this group of artists was Pablo Picasso.

Pablo and Frida became friends. The Louvre Museum bought one of Frida's paintings. She was not used to selling her paintings. Until then, she had given her work away to her friends. Having one of her paintings exhibited in one of the most important museums in the world made her very happy.

Self-Portrait with Monkeys, 1943
Frida Kahlo

Me and My Doll, 1937
Frida Kahlo

Self-Portrait Dedicated to Marte R. Gómez, 1946
Frida Kahlo

In time Frida became increasingly famous. Her paintings were exhibited in a number of museums, and her success abroad became known in Mexico. However, Frida was not happy because Diego Rivera had asked her for a divorce.

Without Diego, Frida had to work hard to support herself. She taught painting at a public school. This work with children and young people helped her recover from her divorce.

When she wasn't able to travel to Mexico City because she wasn't feeling well, her students would come to the Blue House in Coyoacán for their lessons. They loved Frida so much that they called themselves "The Fridos."

Frida and Diego were married a second time and lived together in Coyoacán. She continued to paint. During this time, she painted *Long Live Life* (1954), which became the last painting she completed before her death.

In 1953, Frida had her first one-woman show in Mexico. By then she was very ill. On opening night, her health took a turn for the worse, but she decided to attend anyway. An ambulance transported her to the gallery in her bed. She was able to greet her friends and enjoy the event.

Frida standing before the mirror in the patio at the Blue House, c. 1945-1947
Photo by Lola Álvarez Bravo

Long Live Life, 1954
Frida Kahlo

In 1954, Frida died in that same bed, there at the Blue House, where she had experienced both the best and the worst moments of her life.

Double Portrait: Diego and I,1, 1944
Frida Kahlo

Frida and Diego were divorced.
Later, they remarried.

Frida in her bedroom in the Blue House, c. 1945-1947
Photo by Lola Álvarez Bravo

I LOOK AT YOUR FACE, FRIDA

F. Isabel Campoy
Alma Flor Ada

Look, Frida, look at your face,
look at your face so blue.
Your life has been a shawl of pain
wrapping itself around you.

Look at your face and paint
the thinnest of paper smiles,
that all who see you might drink
the honey that fills your eyes.

I gaze upon your face, Frida,
time and time again.
In it I find a star,
a star and an artist's brush.

A wish journeys upstream
aboard a paper ship,
spreading your love
*   and enormous faith*
to all along the way.

Frida Kahlo, c. 1938-1939
Photo by Nickolas Muray

César Chávez

From a very early age, César Chávez had to help his family.

Farm workers walk under the hot sun
with sweat pouring from their foreheads.
Three hundred miles is a long distance to go on foot.

They are walking from Delano to Sacramento,
California. The march was organized by their leaders,
César Chávez and Dolores Huerta.

The farm workers want everybody to know that their working
conditions are very difficult and unjust.

They want better treatment from the owners
of the fields.

They want justice.

The laws of the state of California are made at the Capitol building in Sacramento.

Martin Luther King, Jr. and Mahatma Gandhi were two great leaders. Both were pacifists. They used *non-violence* in demanding reforms for their people.

César Chávez admir these two leaders.

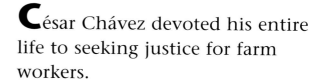
I have a connection because my dad worked many

César Chávez devoted his entire life to seeking justice for farm workers.

He believed in non-violence. He struggled persistently, but peacefully, in favor of farm workers.

struggle was fought with als, strikes, boycotts, marches, theater, and speeches.

he did obtain justice by means, he would fast. He days and days without eating. This was a way to attract the attention of the newspapers and the public.

In 1968, he risked his life by not eating for thirty-six days.

He fasted to protest the use of pesticides which are harmful to the health of farm workers, consumers, and the environment.

Pesticides are poisons that kill the insects that damage crops. Pesticides are harmful to people and to the environment. If a bird eats insects that are poisoned by pesticides, it will lay defective eggs. These eggs will break before the chicks are ready to hatch.

In 1968, César Chávez went on a hunger strike. Here he is with his mother, Juana Chávez, and Senator Robert F. Kennedy after having fasted for twenty-five days.

To understand César Chávez's life, we need to know his background.

In 1909, Cesario and Dorotea Chávez, César Chávez's grandparents, moved to Yuma, Arizona, with their fourteen children.

They came from Chihuahua, Mexico.

One of their fourteen children, Librado, married Juana Estrada in 1924. She was also from Chihuahua.

Librado and Juana had a little store where they sold groceries in Yuma. Their second son, César Estrada Chávez, was born there on March 31, 1927.

Librado and Juana worked very hard, and their business grew. But in 1930, there were many economic problems in the United States. Everybody suffered a lot. That period is known as the *Great Depression*.

During the years of the Great Depression, few people had work or money. Many families moved to California in the hopes of finding work in the fields.

César Chávez with his sister Rita

In 1909, when César Chávez's grandparents arrived in Yuma, Arizona, from Chihuahua, Mexico, Arizona was not a state. It was a "territory." Like Texas and California, Arizona had been a part of Mexico.

[handwritten note:] I difiked that he he had to move to dif. school

César Chávez's family lost their land because they couldn't pay their taxes.

They moved to California to search for work as migrant farm workers.

Sometimes they lived in their car. Other times they lived in tents or in shacks provided by the owners of the fields.

It was a hard life. César attended at least thirty different schools. It was very difficult to study under those conditions.

In the eigth grade, he stopped going to school and began working to help his family.

Migrant farm workers don't own any land. They pick crops or do other jobs wherever they are needed. They spend a few weeks in one place, and when there is no more work there they must go find work elsewhere.

Helen Fabela Chávez always worked very hard. From an early age, she worked the fields and in a grocery store. She had eight children, and she took good care of them and made sure they received an education. She was also active in the United Farm Workers of America.

When César was 15 years old, he met Helen Fabela in Delano, California.

Helen was born in California, but her parents were from Mexico.

Two years later, when he was 17 years old, César joined the navy during World War II.

When he returned to California, César worked in the fields as a farm worker. In 1948, he married Helen, and they went to live in San José, California.

César and Helen lived in a very poor neighborhood called *Sal si puedes* ("Get out if you can").

There they met Fred Ross, who came to speak about the Community Services Organization (CSO).

The main goal of the Community Services Organization was to help Mexican-Americans. Above all, it wanted to help them to register to vote. They believed that voting would help Mexican-Americans obtain better living conditions.

Dolores Huerta is a strong leader of the United Farm Workers. She was the first vice-president of the union and now is the treasurer. She has done an extraordinary job of organizing the union and has never stopped fighting for others. She is the mother of eleven children, two of whom have worked for the union movement.

The farm workers adopted the Aztec eagle as their symbol. It is a symbol of strength because the eagle is a very strong bird. It is a symbol of hope, the hope of rising and flying high.

In the Community Services Organization, (CSO), César and Helen met Dolores Huerta.

For the rest of their lives, César and Dolores worked for justice for farm workers as leaders of the Mexican-American community.

They both worked for the CSO and learned many community organizing techniques.

César and Dolores wanted to create a union that focused on defending farm workers. They left the CSO to form their own National Farm Workers Association (NFWA), which later became the United Farm Workers of America (UFW).

The farm workers' union has the important task of helping farm workers enjoy the same rights as other workers.

When there is no union, some owners of the fields commit many abuses.

In some cases, they do not pay farm workers fairly or do not give them what they offered in the first place.

Before the union was formed, there were no restrooms or water available in the fields.

The camps where farm workers were forced to live were miserable, and conditions were horrible.

Farm workers had no days off and no medical insurance.

If a farm worker was injured or became ill, his or her family was left with nothing to eat.

The union wanted to stop the use of a short-handled hoe. Landowners required that farm workers use this tool. A short-handled hoe forced workers to bend over all day long, and this injured their backs.

Life in the camps was hard. For housing, workers had simple tents or flimsy buildings with dirt floors. There was no running water, nor electricity or bathrooms. Even today, many farm workers live under extremely difficult conditions.

César and the actor Martin Sheen in a march that called for a boycott against grapes.

César Chávez and Dolores Huerta spoke to the Owners, who mostly ignored their requests.

Then they decided to organize marches and boycotts so that the public would know what was happening.

In California, the grape growers didn't pay a fair wage. César and Dolores traveled all over the country speaking out about these problems.

Many people stopped buying grapes and wine from California to help the workers. This forced the owners to pay the workers a fair wage.

During a boycott, the public doesn't buy a certain product so that owners lose money.

Planting and harvesting a crop of grapes is very demanding work. After five years, the boycott resulted in improved working conditions for many farm workers.

César Chávez achieved something that seemed impossible.

It was very difficult to organize farm workers who were constantly moving in search of work.

It was very difficult to ask for contributions from families who were poor.

It was very difficult to respond to violence in a peaceful manner.

César Chávez devoted his whole life to this cause.

His homes, first in Delano, California, and later on in La Paz, Baja California, were always very simple. All the money he collected was turned over to the union.

The union paid for his home and food, but his salary was only ten dollars per month.

The Farm Workers' Theater, *Teatro Campesino*, directed by Luis Valdez, has provided valuable support for the union. This theater group has created and staged plays about the life of farm workers.

Many performers have helped the farm workers' cause. Joan Baez, a famous singer of Mexican-American descent, used her talents to help the cause.

César and Helen
Chávez, with
six of their eight
children.

Helen and César's eight children grew up, studied, and have actively participated in the work of the union and in political struggles over farm workers' rights.

Four of them—Linda, Paul, Liz, and Anthony—have also devoted their lives to the union.

The eldest, Fernando, is a lawyer and was president of the Mexican-American Political Action Association.

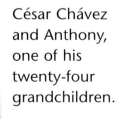

César Chávez
and Anthony,
one of his
twenty-four
grandchildren.

César Chávez died on April 23, 1993. He was sixty-six years old.

After his death, Dolores Huerta promised that the struggle begun by César Chávez would not die with him.

More than forty thousand people attended his funeral.

The union continues its struggle.

One of the union's biggest concerns is that many farm workers' children have cancer.

The union believes that the cancer is caused by the pesticides used in the fields.

Many schools now bear the name of César Chávez. It is a way to honor the memory of this great man. It is also a way to remind children and all people that, YES, YOU CAN DO IT!

This beautiful mural is at César Chávez School in San Francisco, California.

In addition to the many schools that are named after him, there are also many streets and parks named César Chávez. All of these places remind us of this extraordinary man.

The struggle is not over.

To this day, many farm workers are still paid very little for difficult work that nobody else wants to do.

Although farm workers provide us with the food we need to live, their lives continue to be very hard.

During the harvest season, many farm workers live in their cars or in camps with inhuman conditions.

Many need their children to work in the fields instead of going to school, in order to help support the family.

Farm workers often become ill as the result of having to bathe in contaminated water.

We need to open our hearts to farm workers and support their struggle until justice is obtained.

On August 8, 1994, César Chávez received the Presidential Medal of Freedom posthumously. President Clinton delivered the medal to the Chávez family at the White House.

César Chávez deserves many honors. He has received much recognition after his death.

We all feel proud that the Mexican government in 1990 granted him its highest honor, the Aztec Eagle. We also feel proud that the United States has honored him with the Presidential Medal of Freedom.

In 1998, César Chávez became part of the Hall of Fame of the United States Department of Labor.

ACKNOWLEDGEMENTS

Page 5 / Portrait of José Martí by Herman Norrman, 1891. Photo provided by Cuban Heritage Collection, Otto G. Richter Library, University of Miami, Coral Gables, Florida.

Page 19 / Frida Kahlo, 1939. Photo by Nickolas Muray, provided by Biblioteca de las Artes / Centro Nacional de las Artes, Mexico City.

Page 20 / Interior of the Blue House, in Coyoacán, Mexico City, 1949. Museo Frida Kahlo Collection. Photo provided by Biblioteca de las Artes / Centro Nacional de las Artes, Mexico City.

Page 21 / Frida Kahlo at age three, 1910. Photo by Guillermo Kahlo provided by Biblioteca de las Artes / Centro Nacional de las Artes, Mexico City.

Page 21 / Cristina, Adriana, Matilde and Frida Kahlo, c. 1919. Photo by Guillermo Kahlo provided by Biblioteca de las Artes / Centro Nacional de las Artes, Mexico City. Raquel Tibol Collection.

Page 21 / Frida Kahlo, *Portrait of My Father, Wilhelm Kahlo (Retrato de mi padre, Wilhelm Kahlo)*, 1952. Museo Frida Kahlo Collection. Copyright © 2000 Reproduction authorized by the Instituto Nacional de Bellas Artes y Literatura and Banco de México, Fiduciario en el Fideicomiso relativo a los Museos Diego Rivera y Frida Kahlo.

Page 22 / Alejandro Gómez Arias, c. 1928. Photo provided by Biblioteca de las Artes / Centro Nacional de las Artes, Mexico City.

Page 22 / Frida Kahlo, *Frida in Coyoacán (Frida en Coyoacán)*, c. 1927. Copyright © 2000 Reproduction authorized by the Instituto Nacional de Bellas Artes y Literatura and Banco de México, Fiduciario en el Fideicomiso relativo a los Museos Diego Rivera y Frida Kahlo.

Page 22 / Frida Kahlo, *The Bus (El camión)*, 1929. Dolores Olmedo Collection. Copyright © 2000 Reproduction authorized by the Instituto Nacional de Bellas Artes y Literatura and Banco de México, Fiduciario en el Fideicomiso relativo a los Museos Diego Rivera y Frida Kahlo.

Page 23 / Frida Kahlo, *Accident (Accidente)*, 1926. Rafael Coronel Collection. Copyright © 2000 Reproduction authorized by the Instituto Nacional de Bellas Artes y Literatura and Banco de México, Fiduciario en el Fideicomiso relativo a los Museos Diego Rivera y Frida Kahlo.

Page 23 / Frida Kahlo, *Self-Portrait Wearing a Velvet Dress (Autorretrato con traje de terciopelo)*, 1926. Copyright © 2000 Reproduction authorized by the Instituto Nacional de Bellas Artes y Literatura and Banco de México, Fiduciario en el Fideicomiso relativo a los Museos Diego Rivera y Frida Kahlo.

Page 24 / Frida Kahlo, *Frida and Diego (Frida y Diego)*, 1931. Copyright © 2000 Reproduction authorized by the Instituto Nacional de Bellas Artes y Literatura and Banco de México, Fiduciario en el Fideicomiso relativo a los Museos Diego Rivera y Frida Kahlo.

Page 24 / Frida Kahlo, c. 1931. Photo by Imogen Cunningham provided by Biblioteca de las Artes / Centro Nacional de las Artes, Mexico City. Copyright © The Imogen Cunningham Trust.

Page 25 / Frida Kahlo, *Portrait of Dr. Leo Eloesser (Retrato del Dr. Leo Eloesser)*, 1931. Copyright © 2000 Reproduction authorized by the Instituto Nacional de Bellas Artes y Literatura and Banco de México, Fiduciario en el Fideicomiso relativo a los Museos Diego Rivera y Frida Kahlo.

Page 25 / Diego Rivera and Frida Kahlo, c. 1929. Photo provided by Biblioteca de las Artes / Centro Nacional de las Artes, Mexico City.

Page 26 / Matilde and Guillermo Kahlo wedding. Photo provided by Biblioteca de las Artes / Centro Nacional de las Artes, Mexico City.

Page 26 / Diego Rivera, *Detroit Industry* (detail), 1932-33. The Detroit Institute of Arts, Detroit, Michigan. Copyright © 2000 Reproduction authorized by the Instituto Nacional de Bellas Artes y Literatura and Banco de México, Fiduciario en el Fideicomiso relativo a los Museos Diego Rivera y Frida Kahlo.

Page 26 / Frida Kahlo, *Self-Portrait on the Border Between Mexico and the United States (Autorretrato de pie en la frontera México-Estados Unidos)*, 1932. Manuel Reyere Collection. Copyright © 2000 Reproduction authorized by the Instituto Nacional de Bellas Artes y Literatura and Banco de México, Fiduciario en el Fideicomiso relativo a los Museos Diego Rivera y Frida Kahlo.

Page 28 / Frida Kahlo, *Self-Portrait with Monkeys (Autorretrato con simios)*, 1943. Copyright © 2000 Reproduction authorized by the Instituto Nacional de Bellas Artes y Literatura and Banco de México, Fiduciario en el Fideicomiso relativo a los Museos Diego Rivera y Frida Kahlo.

Page 28 / Frida Kahlo, *Me and My Doll (Yo y mi muñeca)*, 1937. Gelman Collection. Copyright © 2000 Reproduction authorized by the Instituto Nacional de Bellas Artes y Literatura and Banco de México, Fiduciario en el Fideicomiso relativo a los Museos Diego Rivera y Frida Kahlo.

Page 29 / Frida Kahlo, *Self-Portrait Dedicated to Marte R. Gómez (Autorretrato dedicado a Marte R. Gómez)*, 1946. Copyright © 2000 Reproduction authorized by the Instituto Nacional de Bellas Artes y Literatura and Banco de México, Fiduciario en el Fideicomiso relativo a los Museos Diego Rivera y Frida Kahlo.

Page 30 / Frida Kahlo, c. 1945-47. Photo by Lola Álvarez Bravo provided by Biblioteca de las Artes / Centro Nacional de las Artes, Mexico City.

Page 30 / Frida Kahlo, *Long Live Life (Viva la vida)*, 1954. Museo Frida Kahlo Collection. Copyright © 2000 Reproduction